Original title:
Sometimes Life Is Just Pizza

Copyright © 2025 Creative Arts Management OÜ
All rights reserved.

Author: Atticus Thornton
ISBN HARDBACK: 978-1-80566-078-1
ISBN PAPERBACK: 978-1-80566-373-7

Unraveled Layers

In the oven, things go round,
Crusty edges, golden brown.
Toppings dance, they shimmy close,
Slice my heart, I love you most.

Cheese that stretches, a gooey show,
Pepperoni in a perfect row.
An artful mess, a tasty scene,
Shall we share? I see what you mean.

Warm Bites in the Cold

Winter winds, they chill the soul,
But here's a slice to make me whole.
Heat escapes with every bite,
Cheesy goodness, pure delight.

Snowflakes fall, I laugh and sing,
Melted cheese is my true king.
Grab a slice, let joy ignite,
Pizza warms a frosty night.

Culinary Dreams

In my dreams, I toss the dough,
Pineapple, no? Let's go with flow.
A sprinkle here, a dash of that,
Flavor explosions, fancy that!

Tomato sauce, a vibrant hue,
In my chef's hat, I rule the crew.
Dreams of toppings, wild and free,
A culinary fantasy.

A Treasure of Tastes

Treasure map for food divine,
X marks the spot – it's pizza time!
Each slice is gold, a savory find,
Taking bites, I leave cares behind.

Basil leaves, the scent so bright,
Amaze my senses every night.
In this world, I'm rich, not poor,
With every crunch, I ask for more.

Cheesy Revelations

Crusty dreams in the oven, hot,
Toppings scattered, a tasty plot.
Saucy whispers, a slice to share,
Baking laughs, with gooey care.

Cheddar chats as we slice and serve,
Life's a mix, full of zest and verve.
Pepperoni hopes, ambitious and bold,
Each bite a story, delightfully told.

Doughy twists of fate arise,
Hilarious toppings, oh what a surprise.
Life's funny moments, cheesy and bright,
In this kitchen, everything feels right.

So grab a fork, let's dig on in,
With every slice, we surely win.
For in this feast, we find our glee,
A belly full of laughs, just like pizza, you see.

Around the Table of Life

Gather 'round the table, come take a seat,
With crusty opinions and spicy heat.
Salty tales and sweet delight,
In this banquet, everything's just right.

Saucy debates on toppings galore,
Who put pineapple? Let's settle the score.
Laughter bubbles from deep within,
As we pass the slices and dive right in.

Dough flops and kitchen blunders too,
Life's like a pizza, it's always askew.
Baked with humor, love, and some care,
A sprinkle of joy is found everywhere.

When the oven sings and delights unfold,
Each shared moment is like pure gold.
So raise a slice, let worries cease,
In this wild feast, we find our peace.

Stories Baked into Dough

In a world where toppings dance,
Crusts tell tales of chance.
Cheese drips like secret schemes,
Slice of life in savory dreams.

Olives act like little eyes,
Watching laughter rise and fly.
Sauce spills stories, thick and bold,
Every bite's a treasure told.

The Poetry of Pizza

Oh, the sonnet of the crust,
Golden edges, oh so just.
Pepperoni rhymes in sync,
A tasty verse, don't you think?

Each slice a stanza, stacked with care,
Melted cheese, a creamy affair.
When hunger strikes, I'm never late,
A pizza pie, my heart does sate.

The Crunch That Comforts

A crust that crackles, soft yet strong,
In every bite, I hum along.
Crispy edges, warm delight,
An instant smile in every bite.

Garlic whispers, herbs that jest,
With each slice, I feel so blessed.
The laughter shared, the crumbs we trade,
In cheesy warmth, our worries fade.

Escaping with Every Bite

Doughy escapes on Tuesday night,
Toppings twirl under the light.
A journey starts with every slice,
Adventure wrapped in cheesy ice.

From pepperoni plains to green bell skies,
I sail away with each surprise.
In every bite, a giggle rings,
As pizza dreams take flight on wings.

Toppings of Tomorrow

When cheese is melting under sun's bright glare,
The toppings dance in my culinary affair.
Olives, peppers, and a sprinkle of glee,
Each slice a promise, oh how good it could be!

Oregano whispers secrets from afar,
While pepperoni dreams of a pizza bazaar.
A crusty fortune, all baked in delight,
With every bite, I feel the future's bite!

Craving the Ordinary

A circle of joy served hot on a plate,
In the world of toppings, I find my fate.
Saucy adventures, all dressed up in gold,
As I dive into flavors so daringly bold!

The mundane magic, a wondrous delight,
Cold pizza in morning, a breakfast in sight.
With each bite I take, I forget all my woes,
In this crusty paradise, anything goes!

Doughy Moments

Dough that rises like my hopes each day,
Kneaded with laughter, tossed worries away.
A sprinkle of flour, a dash of pure fun,
In this round world, I'm never outdone!

My oven's a portal to happiness warm,
Slicing through chaos, it's my culinary charm.
The joy in each piece, carefree and bright,
In this doughy adventure, everything's right!

Saucy Serenade

Oh, the tangy sauce sings a sweet serenade,
Under the moonlight, my taste buds invade.
Basil and garlic join in the song,
Together they celebrate, where flavors belong!

A slice of affection, a loving embrace,
In cheese-dripping moments, I find my place.
Let each bite be a laugh, a silly delight,
In a world topped with joy, everything's bright!

Sauced with Laughter

In a world of cheese and crust,
We find our joy, it's a must.
With each slice, our worries fade,
Pizza parties are perfectly made.

Toppings piled high, what a sight,
Pineapple dreams, oh what a fright!
But we laugh and take a bite,
In this cheesy world, all feels right.

Silent debates on what to choose,
Mushrooms, peppers, or just plain snooze?
With every slice, we break the rules,
Pizza brings joy, we're all just fools.

So raise a slice, let laughter flow,
In this cheesy land, we steal the show.
For with each bite, we freely roam,
In the doughy embrace, we feel at home.

Whispers of Basil and Oregano

In the oven, the magic swirls,
Basil dances, and pepperoni twirls.
With each fragrant breath we take,
A culinary promise, we make.

Crusty chants and cheesy songs,
Making memories that last long.
Who knew dinner could be so fun,
With laughter rising, like the sun?

Saucy stories drip and spill,
Fingers sticky, hearts to fill.
A slice of joy, oh my, oh wow,
Who needs forks? Let's dig in now!

As we munch and chat away,
The world outside can fade away.
In every bite, a funny tale,
With pizza magic, we shall not fail.

Pizza-Fueled Hopes

In a box, the dreams reside,
A cheesy slice, a tasty ride.
With each layer, our spirits rise,
In pepperoni we see the skies.

From crusty thoughts, new plans emerge,
With every bite, we feel the surge.
A sprinkle here, a dash of zest,
With pizza power, we are blessed.

Gather 'round, it's time to cheer,
For every slice, we draw near.
Laughter echoes, love does bloom,
In this pizza land, there's always room.

With laughter shared, and plans begun,
Life is better, oh what fun!
We'll toast our cheer, that tasty dough,
Fueled by hope, we let it flow.

The Warm Embrace of Dough

In the kitchen, magic brews,
A warm embrace in cheesy hues.
Rolling dough and laughter blend,
In this world, our hearts ascends.

Oven heat like summer's glow,
Baking dreams in a tasty show.
With friends beside and smiles so wide,
Pizza's warmth is our joyride.

Crust so soft, it hugs us tight,
In every slice, the world feels right.
Toppings collide, a glorious mess,
Life's a feast, no need to stress.

So slice it up, let giggles reign,
With every bite, we feel no pain.
In the warm embrace, we're never alone,
Pizza's our kingdom, and we call it home.

Personal Pan Paradigms

In a box, my dreams reside,
Cheese and sauce, my trusty guide.
Crusty edges, golden brown,
Slice of joy, never a frown.

Toppings dance in tasty flair,
Pepperoni almost everywhere.
Each bite sings a happy tune,
Laughter shared with fork and spoon.

Life can twist like dough in hands,
A sprinkle here, a dash of bands.
With every slice, a moment cheered,
Pizza wisdom, life endeared.

So grab a slice, don't be shy,
Savor toppings, reach for the sky.
As long as cheese and crust combine,
Everyday joy feels just divine.

The Flavor of Being

Life's a pie, a saucy base,
With every bite, a cheesy grace.
Toppings juggled, wild and free,
On this plate, pure ecstasy.

One slice spicy, one slice sweet,
In this café, we find our beat.
Margherita dreams or rooftop stacks,
Smiles grow wide; who needs the snacks?

Crusts of laughter, bites of bliss,
A perfect meal, we can't dismiss.
Each meal's a tale, yet untold,
Adventures found in crusts of gold.

So come and feast, don't be late,
In this kitchen, celebrate fate.
With laughter and joy, we're truly alive,
In every slice, together we thrive.

Birthdays, Births, and Bites

Candles flicker on the crust,
Wishes made; in pizza we trust.
Every party, a cheesy affair,
Slice of happiness fills the air.

Toppings piled, oh what a sight,
Friends gathered 'round, pure delight.
Each birthday song, a tasty cheer,
A moment served, as joy draws near.

With every bite, memories grow,
Candles snuffed, with each fiery blow.
Barbecued dreams, or veggie bliss,
In every slice, a piece of this.

So let's embrace the cheesy cheer,
On our plates, together we steer.
Birthdays, births, forever we dine,
In the flavors, everything's fine.

Kneaded Moments of Togetherness

Flour on hands, laughter around,
Kneading dough, a joy profound.
Sauce on fingers, stories unfold,
In this kitchen, our hearts turn gold.

On rainy days, we toss and spin,
Tossing dough up, let the fun begin.
Friendship baked with every spice,
Together we feast; oh, how nice!

Crusty hearts and melted joy,
In every slice, a favorite ploy.
Slice it up, share the thrill,
Kneaded moments that fit the bill.

So gather near, let's make a feast,
In every bite, joy will increase.
In the warmth of laughter, we remain,
Baked in joy, love, and plain.

A Feast of Dreams

In the oven, hopes do rise,
Cheesy dreams beneath the skies.
Toppings dance, a joyous sight,
Each slice served brings delight.

Crusty edges, golden brown,
With every bite, I wear my crown.
Saucy stories, laughter shared,
A banquet where no one is scared.

Glimpse a pepperoni star,
Sharing slices near and far.
In this feast of simple cheer,
Every gathering draws us near.

With a sprinkle of good humor,
Each laugh's a tasty rumor.
Let's toast a slice to every friend,
In this feast, the joy won't end.

Morsels of Memory

Childhood days, crusts torn apart,
Tomato stains on my brave heart.
Bites of laughter, cheesy games,
Each memory, a flavor claims.

Gathered 'round the table wide,
A treasure trove we can't hide.
With every slice, a tale unfolds,
Morsels of memory, pure gold.

Pizza night with friends so dear,
Sharing laughter, never fear.
Silly toppings, where we roam,
Each slice reminds us, we're at home.

From the greasy to the gourmet,
Every bite finds its own way.
In the crust lies our delight,
Morsels keep our hearts so light.

Flavors of Tomorrow

In the kitchen, dreams align,
Pepper flakes and herbs entwine.
Dough rising like my hopes high,
In every slice, a future pie.

Gooey layers, vibrant hues,
Endless choices, clever views.
What's today's special, I must ask,
A tasty future, quite the task!

Think beyond the simple cheese,
Bite into life with such ease.
Savor the moments, let them flow,
Each slice a spark, a chance to grow.

With friends beside, we take a bite,
Flavors mingle, pure delight.
In every crust, a path we see,
To tomorrow's dreams, wild and free.

The Art of Savoring

Each slice a canvas, toppings rare,
Artistry baked with love and care.
Fold it gently, take a pause,
Savor the moment, just because.

A drizzle here, a sprinkle there,
Life's little details, beyond compare.
With each bite, I celebrate,
The art of savoring my fate.

Laughing friends, a vibrant scene,
Chewy crust, and flavors keen.
In the tapestry of joy we share,
Every slice is a love affair.

So raise a glass, let laughter ring,
In every slice, let your heart sing.
Artful reminders of joy and cheer,
In every assembly, love is clear.

A Palette of Flavor

Cheese slides in a cheesy grin,
Toppings dance, let the feast begin.
Crust so golden, a warm embrace,
Each bite taken, a happy face.

Pepperoni winks from the side,
Mushrooms laugh, there's no need to hide.
Sauce like a river, rich and bold,
A slice of joy, a story told.

Pineapple brings a tropical flair,
While olives share secrets with air.
A party on a plate, oh so bright,
A culinary joy, pure delight.

The flavors blend, a symphony's play,
In the kitchen, it's a grand ballet.
So when life's tough, take a slice—
For joy can come in cheesy rice!

The Harmony of the Oven

In the oven, dreams start to rise,
Dough spins around under watchful eyes.
A sprinkle of spices, a dash of zest,
Creating a pie that's simply the best.

Bakes with a giggle, the timer's chime,
A melody formed, a rhythm of thyme.
The crust sings sweet songs of the heat,
As aromas twist, a savory treat.

Friends gathered round, laughter galore,
Each slice served up brings joy to the floor.
With each little nibble, we all feel blessed,
In this warm world, we're truly caressed.

The oven hums softly, a lullaby,
As we savor each bite, and dreams start to fly.
In every crust, there's a memory spun,
In harmony with flavors, life's just begun.

Sharing Plates and Stories

Gather 'round, the table set,
Each slice reveals a happy duet.
As we share our tales over cheese,
Life's great moments are sure to please.

Tomato tales and garlic jokes,
Running wild with laughter provokes.
In the midst of joy, we find our spark,
In cheesy debates, we leave a mark.

Crusts are broken, stories flow,
With every slice, our hearts aglow.
A sprinkle of good cheer on each dish,
With every story shared, we've grown rich.

So let's toast with crust and toppings bright,
To the flavors that make our lives feel right.
In every gathering, laughter's the key,
For sharing plates holds the sweetest glee.

The Whisker's Journey

A little whisker wandered wide,
On a quest for toppings, pure and fried.
Through twisted alleys and cheesy lanes,
Seeking out flavors in spicy veins.

With a garlic clove as a trusty friend,
They journeyed onward, around each bend.
A sprinkle of herbs, a dash of fun,
In the world of pizza, they would run.

Through kitchens bustling, dough would fly,
As pans clanged loud, they'd laugh and sigh.
The scents of basil, a siren call,
In every bite, they'd risk it all.

So raise your slice, let's celebrate,
All the whiskers chasing their fate.
For in every journey, fun's in the feast,
In the world of flavors, we're truly released.

Saucy Inspirations

A doughy base, a cheesy cheer,
Toppings tossed without a fear.
Olives smile, and peppers dance,
In this feast, our hearts enhance.

A sprinkle here, a drizzle there,
Forks and knives flying everywhere.
We laugh at slices, crusts like crowns,
In this kitchen, joy abounds.

Banana peppers in a twist,
It's a party not to be missed.
Bite the crust as laughter swells,
Every chew, a secret tells.

A Canvas of Flavor

Colorful toppings jam-packed tight,
Each slice reveals a new delight.
Tomatoes shout in bold red hues,
A symphony of taste to choose.

A canvas bright, a mosaic feast,
Pepperoni joins with zest unleashed.
In every fold, surprise awaits,
A masterpiece on dinner plates.

Baked with love, a golden glow,
Sausage winks, it's quite the show.
Folks gather round, with eyes so wide,
As flavors mingle, joy won't hide.

Crusty Connections

Friends around a table wide,
With crusty dreams, we all abide.
Each shared slice, a hearty laugh,
A little cheese to soothe the path.

In the oven, warmth does rise,
As the scent fills up the skies.
Saucy stories, one by one,
In a cheesy world, we're all just fun.

From thin to thick, we make amends,
In the sauce, we find our friends.
Life is better when we share,
With every bite, we show we care.

Life on a Plate

A plate adorned with joy and glee,
Flavors mingle, wild and free.
Garlic breath and smiles wide,
In this feast, our hearts collide.

Crust and topping, side by side,
Through the laughter, we will glide.
When the heat brings us so near,
An extra slice, let's raise a cheer!

Every morsel tells a tale,
Of adventures never stale.
In this moment, we unite,
Pizza love, our shared delight.

When the Sauce Meets the Spirit

In a world of toppings bright,
We dance with flavors, what a sight.
From pepperoni to green delight,
We laugh, we feast, into the night.

A joke on crust, it cracks a smile,
Each bite we take, we savor style.
With garlic knots that take a while,
We celebrate, it's all worthwhile.

A sprinkle here, a dash of cheer,
In doughy dreams, we have no fear.
Join the party, pizza near,
With every slice, we shed a tear.

So grab a plate, let laughter spin,
In cheese and sauce, we dive right in.
This joyous feast, where dreams begin,
The slice of life, we'll always win.

A Slice of Everyday Magic

Beneath the oven's warmth so bright,
A world awakens, pure delight.
Tomato dreams in every bite,
We dance around the table's light.

Sausage sings a merry tune,
While mushrooms caper, like a boon.
In cheesy bliss, we find our groove,
With every slice, we find our move.

Each crusty edge, a tale to tell,
Of doughy battles fought so well.
A sprinkle here, a laugh to quell,
With every bite, we bid farewell.

So raise a slice to daily thrills,
In peppered joy, our laughter spills.
With friends around and tasty fills,
This magic pizza always chills.

Doughy Delights in the Chaos

In the kitchen, chaos reigns,
Flour storms and wild grains.
Rolling out with giggling strains,
A doughy ballet, no restraints.

With pepper flakes and sauce galore,
Laughter echoes, we'll explore.
Each topping fight is never a bore,
In cheesy dreams, we always soar.

The pizza spins, a circus act,
It flies and twirls, what a fact!
In this madness, joy is packed,
A crown of herbs, deliciously stacked.

So grab a slice, it's time to feast,
In silly antics, we're released.
With cheesy goodness, love increased,
In every bite, we are the beast.

Cheese Melts and Heartfelt Turns

As cheese melts on a crusty bed,
We chat and laugh, our worries shed.
A sprinkle of joy, a rise ahead,
In every slice, sweet tales are bred.

With each new bite, our hearts entwine,
In tasty pools, our spirits shine.
We toast to life, with fizzy wine,
These moments shared, forever mine.

Beneath the sauce, a secret hub,
Of dreams and schemes, we rub-a-dub.
In pizza world, we form a club,
With every slice, we've found our grubs.

So gather 'round, let spirits churn,
In crusty laughs, our hearts will burn.
With cheesy dreams, it's our turn,
In every slice, new love to earn.

Ingredients of Inspiration

Dough rolls down like dreams so wide,
Toppings dance, a joyous ride.
Cheese pulls apart with gooey grace,
Each bite a smile, a warm embrace.

Pepperonis laugh in circles round,
In this plate, pure joy is found.
Basil sprinkles hopes so bright,
Every slice a burst of light.

When Life Gets Saucy

Tomato red, a bold delight,
Spicy tales that ignite the night.
Oven's warmth, a friendly hug,
Sipping drinks, all woes are shrugged.

Crusty edges, tales of fun,
With every bite, we come undone.
In sauce we trust, so rich and thick,
Swirling flavors, a magic trick.

A Feast of Fond Memories

Gather round, the table set,
Laughter shared, we won't forget.
From cheesy chats to crusty tales,
In every slice, nostalgia sails.

Kids with hands full, faces bright,
Graze on goodies throughout the night.
Each topping tells a story, bold,
Flavorful moments, never old.

The Comfort of Every Slice

Warm and cheesy, pure delight,
Bringing smiles through day and night.
Garlic bites and sweet surprise,
Each slice brings comfort, hope that flies.

A crusty shield from life's hard knocks,
Crispy edges like gentle socks.
Gathered close, with hearts at ease,
Every slice a warm, tasty breeze.

The Great Topping Debate of Happiness

In a world of cheese and crust,
Toppings spark the fiercest dust.
Pineapple lovers, bold and bright,
Fight with sausage in delight.

Veggies green and mushrooms brown,
Call each other names, renown.
But in the end, we all agree,
The best slice shared is meant for free.

Pepperoni Dreams and Olive Wishes

Pepperoni dreams on a cheesy floor,
Olive wishes linger, never a bore.
Slices stacked like hopes on high,
In the pizza skies, we laugh and sigh.

With each bite, we laugh and cheer,
Toppings tell tales, all sincere.
Who knew such joy could be so neat,
When crust and toppings dance and meet?

In the Oven of Existence

In the oven, life's a bake,
Heat of laughter, love we make.
Crusty edges, soft inside,
A savory ride, with friends beside.

Timers beep, and moments rise,
Saucy days and cheesy skies.
Slice by slice, we savor glee,
In every bite, pure ecstasy.

Crusty Corners of Contentment

In the crusty corners, joy resides,
With pepper flakes where whimsy hides.
Sauce spills stories, crunchy tales,
Beneath the knife, the laughter trails.

Pizza parties, oh what fun,
Baking under the golden sun.
Slice your worries, pass the cheer,
In these corners, life's so dear.

A Tasty Interpretation of Time

In the oven, moments bake,
Clock hands spin, but we just take.
Slicing hours like pepperoni,
Cheesy laughter, never phony.

Each minute drips with gooey glee,
Tasting life, just you and me.
Crusty memories rise, delight,
Every bite feels just so right.

Saucy Stories of Connection

With every slice, a tale unfolds,
Topped with laughter, heat, and bolds.
Friends gather 'round, oh what a feast,
Saucy moments never cease.

Pepper flakes and spicy dreams,
Chatting 'til the moonlight gleams.
Stories shared like melted cheese,
Life's rich flavor, sure to please.

The Slice that Stopped the Clock

As the timer buzzes, we just smile,
Time stands still for a little while.
A pizza dream on a dinner plate,
Each bite a joy that cannot wait.

With toppings piled high like fun,
The clock is paused, we've finally won.
A moment shared, it feels so sweet,
In the realm of dough, we find our beat.

Sharing Warmth Over Crust

Gather 'round, the dough is warm,
Life's chaos fades, we brace the storm.
Crusty goodness, laughter flows,
In cheesy hugs, friendship grows.

A golden pie brings hearts to cheer,
With every slice, we hold what's dear.
Together we munch, stories alive,
In each tasty bite, we thrive.

Life's Kitchen Symphony

In a kitchen bustling with cheer,
Pans are clanging, let's make it clear.
Tomato sauce splatters the wall,
As my dough starts to do the polka ball.

Cheese rains down like a fluffy snow,
Pepperoni dances, putting on a show.
Garlic knots doing the twist with glee,
In this culinary jamboree!

Ovens hum their warm, sweet song,
Baking delights where we all belong.
Slice it up, share a hearty laugh,
In this pizza party, we're the autograph.

Raise your slice like an old jazz tune,
With every bite, we'll be over the moon.
Gather 'round, in this kitchen divine,
Life's a pizza pie, and it's simply fine!

Doughy Delights

Knead the dough like you mean it, friend,
Roll it out, let the fun not end.
Toss it high into the air,
Flour fights are a tasty affair!

Sauce it up with a big old splash,
Make a masterpiece in a flash.
Olives rolling like little balls,
Watch those toppings bounce and fall!

It's a pie with a colorful flair,
Each slice a treasure—beyond compare.
Grab a plate, don't you dare wait,
In this doughy delight, we all celebrate!

Just one more slice? I won't ask twice,
Every cheesy bite is oh-so-nice.
With friends by your side, dig in with pride,
In this doughy delight, where joy can't hide!

The Flavor of Friendship

In every crust there's a story to share,
Topped with laughter, sprinkled with care.
Cheesy jokes and pepperoni dreams,
Our friendship's as rich as melted creams.

Gather 'round the table, it's time to feast,
Slice up the fun, let worries be ceased.
Pass the garlic knots, don't be shy,
In this melting pot, together we fly!

A pinch of joy, a dash of trust,
Our bonds grow stronger—through cheese and crust.
With each savory bite, we find our way,
In the flavor of friendship, we'll always stay!

So raise your slice, toast to the night,
Every shared laugh makes the heart feel light.
In the oven of life, we bake and blend,
Together forever, on that we depend!

Crusty Adventures

Off on a journey, what will we find?
A crusty map, the big chance to unwind.
Sailing through toppings on a cheese-filled sea,
To find the best slice, just you and me!

A journey through pepperoni peaks,
Exploring the valleys where the mozzarella leaks.
Tangled in toppings, what a grand quest,
For the crispy delights that we cherish the best!

Saucy rivers and cheesy streams,
We'll conquer the world with our pizza dreams.
With every adventure, our friendship will rise,
In this crusty escapade, under tasty skies!

So grab your forks, let's take a bite,
Embrace the flavor, it feels so right.
In every adventure, laughter's the key,
In a world made of pizza, forever we'll be!

A Pie of Possibilities

A round delight on a plate,
With toppings to make you salivate.
From pepperoni to veggie bliss,
Every slice feels like pure happiness.

Chopped up dreams in cheesy swirls,
Baked to perfection, watch it unfurl.
Doughy clouds on a saucy sea,
Every bite just sets you free.

Crusty treasures, crispy and neat,
Life's little wonders beneath each sheet.
Life can be saucy, gooey, and bold,
In every slice, a story unfolds.

So grab a fork, don't hesitate,
In this funny feast, let's celebrate.
With every munch, the world's so bright,
A pie of joy, a delicious bite!

Crust and Comfort

In the oven, warmth is born,
A golden crust, the heart's adorn.
Cheese like sunshine on a rainy day,
A comforting hug in the cheesiest way.

When the day is long and grind is tough,
A pizza slice makes all things buff.
With a side of laughter, life feels right,
Crusty joys, our hearts take flight.

A sprinkle of herbs, a dash of cheer,
In this cheesy realm, there's nothing to fear.
Each slice a smile, each bite a glee,
This round delight is therapy!

So come on friends, gather 'round,
In this pie of joy, our bliss is found.
With doughy dreams and flavors galore,
Life is tasty, who could ask for more?

The Tantalizing Topping

Layers stacked, oh what a treat,
With colorful toppings, the combo's sweet.
Mushrooms and olives dance on cheese,
A whimsical party that aims to please.

From spicy jalapeños that make you sweat,
To pineapple chunks, the ultimate bet.
The more the merrier, that's the rule,
In this zany feast, take a dip in the pool.

Sauce drips down like life's delightful mess,
Making mundane moments feel blessed.
The laughter rises, the party is here,
With every topping, we conquer our fear.

So pile it high, don't hold back,
In this cheesy world, there's no lack.
Each adventure begins with a sing,
In the court of pizza, we're all pawns to fling!

Slices of Serenity

A slice in hand, the world's at bay,
With melted cheese to whisk fears away.
In crusty comfort, we find our peace,
A simple pleasure that will never cease.

The world may spin and life may race,
But here, my friend, we've found our place.
Between the bites, laughter and cheer,
In this shared moment, joy is near.

Twirling toppings on a doughy dance,
Life's silly moments deserve a chance.
With every stitch of savory delight,
We fade to calm, from day to night.

So let us feast, let us chime,
In slices of laughter, we'll pass the time.
A pizza party, where we find our sanity,
Sharing the joy, it's pure humanity!

Cheese-laden Reflections

In the fridge, a treasure waits,
A crusty dream that captivates.
With every slice, my joy ignites,
Cheesy bliss on starry nights.

Tomato sauce like liquid gold,
In each warm bite, a story told.
A sprinkle here, a sprinkle there,
Brings laughter, love, a dash of flair.

A pepperoni dance, oh what a sight,
Twirling around in the warm, dim light.
When life gets tough, I take a bite,
And suddenly, the world's just right.

So grab a slice, let worries flee,
In cheesy goodness, I find glee.
For in this round, delightful treat,
I find the joy, I find the heat.

The Essence of Every Slice

Crust so flaky, toppings divine,
Each mouthful sings, a taste so fine.
A cheesy hug on a plate so round,
In every slice, pure joy is found.

On lazy days or rainy nights,
With friends around, we share delights.
Extra cheese, a habit grand,
In every meal, a caring hand.

From hawaiian dreams to veggie tales,
Life's ups and downs are like these trails.
No matter the toppings, sweet or wild,
Pizza brings out the inner child.

So dance with joy, let laughter throng,
In every bite, we do belong.
Each slice a laugh, a heart's embrace,
In the world of carbs, we've found our place.

Savory Moments

A box arrives, the magic spills,
Warm aroma sends delightful thrills.
With each slice, adventure starts,
A tasty journey that captures hearts.

Garlic knots on the side, oh bliss,
Dip them right, you won't want to miss.
Laughter shared over cheesy bites,
Moments savored, reaching new heights.

Crust so thin, or piled up high,
A guilty pleasure, oh my, oh my!
When troubles come, just take a piece,
In tasty layers, you find your peace.

So gather 'round, let the fun ignite,
With every slice, the world feels bright.
In savory joy, let's lift our voices,
For pizza nights are our best choices.

A Tasty Escape

When life gets wild, I make a plea,
To cheesy wonders calling me.
With pepperoni, onions, and more,
I escape to a pizza paradise shore.

Doughy dreams and toppings galore,
In every piece, laughter we score.
A bite of joy, a slice of glee,
In the world of pizza, I'm truly free.

Forget the stress, let worries fade,
In melted cheese, the world's remade.
With friends surrounding, let's raise a cheer,
For every bite brings love and beer!

Oh, crusty circles of happiness bright,
In every party, you steal the night.
So here's to the joy found in each taste,
In pizza's embrace, our worries erased.

An Ode to the Dough

Beneath the sauce, a crust does rise,
A canvas blank, where dreams can fly.
It holds our hopes, our cheesy wish,
In every slice, a cheesy kiss.

It bends and twists, a shapeshifter's art,
A warm embrace, it tugs the heart.
With flour dreams dusted in the air,
Oh, wondrous dough, beyond compare!

The Simplicity in Each Bite

A simple dish, yet oh so grand,
In every crust, we understand.
With toppings piled, a quirky sight,
Each bite a giggle, pure delight.

From pepperoni to veggie thrills,
It fills our laughs and laughter spills.
A world of flavors in each chew,
Life's little joys served hot and true.

Memories in the Toppings

A sprinkle here, a drizzle there,
Each topping tells a tale to share.
From birthday parties, laughter loud,
To midnight snacks, a cheesy crowd.

An adventure on a crusty base,
Friends gather round, the happy space.
Olives, onions, and peppers bright,
A feast of memories, pure delight!

Melty Moments

Cheese that stretches, oh what a show,
With every pull, the smiles grow.
A symphony of flavors blend,
In every slice, pure joy will send.

The oven hums a song so sweet,
As friends all gather 'round to eat.
With laughter shared, we take a bite,
In melty moments, everything's right.

Topping Each Day

Wake up each morning with a grin,
What shall I add to today's spin?
A sprinkle of cheese, a dash of zest,
Each little topping, I must confess.

With pepperoni dreams swirling around,
In the kitchen, I dance and bound.
Tomatoes line up, so plump, so red,
Garnishing the thoughts in my head.

A crust that's crispy, a crust that's hot,
Life's little flavors, I'll take a plot.
When troubles arise, I roll out the dough,
And savor the moments, just take it slow.

Craving the Crunch

In the fridge awaits a cheesy delight,
A slice of joy, my appetite ignites.
Crunchy shield, golden and bright,
Bite after bite, pure love at first sight.

While others chase dreams, I chase this meal,
A savory treasure, that's oh so surreal.
The rhythm of life, a dance on my plate,
With toppings galore, I just can't wait.

Each bite is laughter, no need for a frown,
As I devour my way through town.
A smile so wide, a heart full of cheer,
Craving that crunch, it's perfectly clear.

Life in a Box

Open the box, what treasure inside?
A medley of colors, where flavors collide.
A slice of adventure, the crust is my guide,
On this cheesy journey, I feel actualized.

Folded in paper, a portable feast,
An edible journey, to say the least.
Friends gathered 'round, laughter in the air,
In the realm of toppings, we haven't a care.

Each slice a story, a giggle, a tale,
With sauce like a canvas, we set our sail.
Life may be messy, but oh what a box,
In moments of cheese, we truly unlock.

A Delicious Distraction

When life gets tangled and the day seems long,
I reach for a slice, where I belong.
Cheesy goodness, a warm embrace,
In each little piece, I find my place.

A sauce-swirled dance beneath the sun,
What's better than this? Oh, what fun!
With each gooey layer, I chuckle and sigh,
A delicious escape, where worries say bye.

Though troubles may simmer like sauce on the flame,
Mouthfuls of joy help me forget the same.
Life's absurdities turn into glee,
With a pizza in hand, I'm wild and free.

Slice by Slice

In a world full of woes, we find delight,
With every warm slice, our hearts take flight.
Cheese stretched like dreams, on a crust so fine,
Sharing this joy, you're forever mine.

Life's a feast, with toppings galore,
Pepperoni laughter and so much more.
With each tasty bite, worries dissolve,
A cheesy embrace, our problems resolve.

Grease stains like memories, smudged on the path,
With every deep dish, we share in the laugh.
Together we gather, our joy so immense,
In this cheesy circle, we build our defense.

So grab a slice, let the good times roll,
Life's best served hot, that's the ultimate goal.
With friends by your side, and the oven's warm kiss,
You'll find in each bite, the taste of pure bliss.

The Pizza Paradox

In a box of surprises, it's all a roulette,
With every new topping, we laugh and we fret.
Should I go Hawaiian or stick with plain?
Life's like a pizza, full of joy and some pain.

A sprinkle of spice, a dash of sweet cheer,
Sausage or mushrooms? Let's tackle that fear.
Each slice a decision, so complex yet bright,
In the oven of fate, we bake what feels right.

Crust so forgiving, it teaches us grace,
To savor each moment, there's no way to replace.
With marinara giggles and mozzarella dreams,
Life's a big pie, bursting at the seams.

So let's slice it up, share laughter and glee,
In this cheesy existence, just you and me.
Whether thin or deep dish, it's all just a game,
In the pizza of life, we're all just the same.

Toppings of Tranquility

In the oven of hopes, our dreams start to rise,
With basil and laughter, we seek no disguise.
Each topping tells stories, each slice a new page,
In the cookbook of chaos, we find our own stage.

From olives to pickles, a curious blend,
Life's a buffet, with flavors to send.
We pile on the laughter, with cheese cascading,
A party of toppings, creativity braiding.

Sauce dripping joy, like secrets we share,
Embrace the absurdity, throw caution to air.
Life's best in the kitchen, where chaos can thrive,
A dash of connection, that's where we arrive.

So roll out your laughter, and knead out the stress,
With each tasty slice, we'll find our own zest.
In this pizzeria world, be bold and be free,
With toppings of joy, become who you'll be.

Doughy Confessions

Underneath the crust, secrets arise,
Each bite is a rumor, no need for disguise.
A sprinkle of truth, a handful of fun,
Adventures in flavor, we'll never outrun.

Cheese tangled in stories, like friends on a spree,
Greasy confessions slip out joyfully.
Through pepperoni tales, we unveil our plight,
In the doughy embrace, everything feels right.

Oven-baked chuckles, the warmth of the crew,
With each crunchy bite, we're forever brand new.
From crust to the edge, life's a savory ride,
Through laughter and toppings, we'll always abide.

So let's raise our slices, a toast with good cheer,
To doughy confessions, we hold oh so dear.
In the kitchen of life, let's dance with delight,
Where every bite shared makes the world feel just right.

Occasionally Cheesy Reconnections

Life is like a dough, so round and warm,
With toppings wild, it takes a form.
Friends may drift, but cheese is glue,
Bringing us back, like it always do.

Under the sauce, old jokes still thrive,
A sprinkle of laughter, we come alive.
Crusty edges hold stories bold,
In every bite, new tales unfold.

Mushrooms dancing on a golden base,
In this pizza party, there's always space.
A dash of garlic, a pinch of flair,
Who knew pizza could bring us so near?

So here's to the slices that bond us tight,
Even when life gets a bit too bright.
Let's raise our crusts to the moments we share,
For in every pizza, there's love in the air.

Slice of the Unexpected

Ordering a pie, what could go wrong?
Ancho chili? Pineapple? That's too strong!
Yet with each bite, a strange delight,
It's the oddest pairings that feel so right.

Life is a menu, a buffet of chances,
Toppings that dance with whimsical glances.
Veggies and meats with flavors unite,
Like mismatched socks, they just feel right.

Under the cheese, surprises await,
No boring slices on this plate.
Each new topping a story unfolds,
In laughter and taste, our joy beholds.

So slice me a piece, let's not delay,
In this unexpected feast, we'll laugh away.
With every crunch, a memory builds,
In the world of pizza, no heart ever stills.

Topped with Joy

A doughy base, so soft and round,
Life's little joys in toppings are found.
With a drizzle of sauce and a sprinkle of cheer,
Each bite is a giggle, oh dear, oh dear!

Olives rolling like tiny black gems,
Amongst the cheese, they make new friends.
Peppers that pop and onions that sing,
In every slice, joy's the main thing.

Crust so fluffy, like pillows of wonder,
Each slice shared pulls us from under.
With laughter and sauces both sweet and bold,
These moments of joy are treasures to hold.

So gather around with your team of delight,
Let's feast on this pizza, a marvelous sight.
In this pizza realm, we align and rejoice,
For happiness comes with a cheesy voice.

Aligning with Pepperoni

In life's pizza oven, we bake and blend,
Pepperoni circles need no amend.
They twist and twirl on a cheesy floor,
Bringing smiles and laughter; who could want more?

Baked to perfection, a feast for the eyes,
A medley of colors, a delicious surprise.
Crusty diplomacy on a plate we bring,
Unity found in every single zing.

From party to party, we gather with glee,
Sharing our slices, just you and me.
The more the toppings, the merrier the tale,
A balancing act, where none shall fail.

So let's raise our slicers and toast with delight,
For in every bite, there's magic in sight.
Aligning with flavors, we find a new way,
From pepperoni circles, joy forever will stay.

Savory Moments in a Doughy Dream

In a world of sauce and cheese,
I find my heart at ease.
Doughy clouds above my head,
Toppings dance, no need for bed.

Life's a slice, a twist of fate,
With pepperoni as my mate.
Beneath the cheese, the joy does melt,
In every bite, pure bliss is felt.

Crusty edges, golden brown,
Worry not, just wear a crown.
Tomato dreams, a savory tease,
Each release brings such sweet ease.

With every fold, a story told,
In this feast, we need not be bold.
Laughs arise with every chew,
Pizza love, that's always true.

Toppings of Joy and Crusty Comfort

With a sprinkle of joy, I feast,
On a slice, my worries cease.
Basil whispers in the air,
Crust so soft, beyond compare.

Mushrooms dance, a merry crew,
Sausage sings, oh how it grew!
In a world of melted dreams,
Happiness flows with gooey streams.

Olives wink, a playful jest,
In this pie, I find my zest.
Each bite filled with tasty cheer,
A circle of laughter, my dear.

Slices shared with friends around,
In this moment, joy is found.
With a wink and cheesy grin,
Let the pizza party begin!

Slices of Serendipity

In the oven, dreams ignite,
Golden crust shines, oh what a sight!
Tomatoes twirl in a saucy dance,
With every bite, I take a chance.

Pizza nights, a joyous spree,
Every flavor sings to me.
On this plate, my worries fade,
In every slice, pure bliss is laid.

Gather 'round, it's time to share,
Cheesy goodness fills the air.
Laughter erupts, a hearty cheer,
As crusty comfort draws us near.

Serendipity on a plate,
With each topping, we celebrate.
In this moment, all is right,
Life's a pizza, pure delight!

Cheesy Whispers of Afternoon Delight

Cheddar dreams in sunny rays,
Melted magic fills my days.
Every slice, a secret told,
In cheesy whispers, hearts unfold.

With every bite, a giggle bursts,
Saucy tales that quench our thirsts.
Spinach smiles and pepper laughs,
In this meal, love's photograph.

Afternoon sun and pizza high,
Chasing clouds that float on by.
Let's relish in this tasty art,
For pizza always warms the heart.

Each topping tells a story bright,
In this feast, we feel our light.
So grab a slice and take a chance,
Join the doughy, happy dance!

Sauced in Serenity

On a Tuesday night, no plans at all,
A hot pie waits, I hear its call.
Cheese stretching like dreams in the air,
Toppings piled high, no room for despair.

The crust is thick, my worries thin,
Each bite brings joy, oh where to begin?
With every slice, I feel so grand,
In this cheesy world, I now make my stand.

Grease drips down, a laugh I share,
A little mess won't cause me to care.
Tomato sauce smiles, a wink from the night,
In this pizza party, everything feels right.

So here's to the laughter, the chaos, the fun,
In a world spinning madly, I'll take a slice run!
With my friends gathered round and joy in the pie,
We feast on absurdity, and let out a cry!

A Palette of Flavors and Fables

Oh, the toppings dance in a colorful show,
Pepperoni twirls; see it steal the glow.
Mushrooms waltz with their earthy grace,
While olives roll in a savory race.

Each slice tells stories of laughter and cheer,
Saucy adventures, let's gather near.
The crust is a canvas, the slices our fate,
In this oven of humor, we celebrate hate.

Cheddar's a joker; it likes to play,
While garlic's the life of the party, they say.
We pile on the toppings, our laughter accumulates,
In this culinary chaos, joy radiates.

So let's dig in and savor the bite,
With a sprinkle of humor, everything feels right.
As we chew through the tales, one slice at a time,
In this pizzeria of dreams, we're all in our prime!

Craving Connection in Every Bite

In a city of hustle, we find our way,
Through cheese-laden journeys, we laugh and play.
Gathering round with friends and a pie,
To share in the flavors, oh me, oh my!

Crusts are our cushions, our hearts on the table,
Each slice a story, each bite a fable.
From BBQ to veggie, we cover the spread,
In this cheesy abode, there's no room for dread.

With laughter rising like dough in the heat,
We pull out the jokes as we gobble and eat.
On peppered adventures, with crusts that unite,
A feast of connection, all feels just right.

So let's savor the moments, each flavor divine,
In this banquet of happiness, everything's fine.
Raise your slices high; let our spirits ignite,
In this pizza romance, we find pure delight!

Calories of Carefree Laughter

Where pizza reigns, we throw caution to fries,
With toppings galore, we banish our sighs.
A sprinkle of joy, a dash of good cheer,
In the kingdom of cheese, there's nothing to fear.

The crust is our buddy, it takes us along,
With each gooey slice, we burst into song.
Sausage and spinach, in collusion they plot,
To fill up our souls, oh they hit the spot!

Each calorie counts in this joyous affair,
We stack up the laughter, with plenty to share.
No guilt on our plates, just a smile and a bite,
In this crispy utopia, everything feels right.

So here's to the moments that spark joy anew,
With toppings galore, our friendship's the glue.
In giggles and slices, we relish the day,
In this cheesy escape, we always will stay!

Cravings that Bind Us

When hunger strikes, we call in haste,
Toppings galore, a cheesy taste.
With friends around, we slice and share,
Our laughter rings, a feast laid bare.

Each bite a smile, each crust a joke,
We argue toppings, a playful poke.
No debates on pineapple, just let it be,
For in this moment, we're all carefree.

Harmony in a Pizza Box.

In a cardboard haven, joy resides,
A circle of happiness that never hides.
Jalapeños dance with pepperoni's thrill,
Sauce cascades down, a perfect spill.

We gather 'round, our plates are set,
With cheesy strings, we won't forget.
Each slice a symphony, a tasty tune,
Baked under the watch of a silvery moon.

Cheese Dreams and Crusty Wishes

A world of cheese, where wishes blend,
In every slice, our cravings mend.
Garlic knots whisper our secret desires,
As we dream of pies, our hearts catch fires.

With every crust, a wish takes flight,
Beneath starlit skies, we feast at night.
Saucy dreams and laughter ensue,
In this pizza land, our joys renew.

A Slice of Solace

When days feel heavy, and troubles weigh,
A hot slice of joy comes to play.
With a twirl of cheese and a glint of crust,
Each bite a reminder of life's simple trust.

In grease we find our friendly moments,
Toppings unite, our sweet torments.
So here's to the joy, the laughter it brings,
In each little slice, our spirit sings.

The Sizzle of Happiness

In a pan, there's a dance of cheese,
Bubbling joy that aims to please.
A sprinkle of herbs, a pinch of spice,
Every slice is a little slice of nice.

Toppings galore, a hodgepodge feast,
From pepperoni to veggies, never ceased.
A surprising crunch with every bite,
Who knew joy could be so light?

Friends gather round, the laughter erupts,
As doughy dreams fill hungry cups.
We share the plates, we share the laughs,
A melt-in-your-mouth kind of photograph.

And when the pizza spins in the air,
It's like our worries don't even care.
So let's get saucy, let's raise a toast,
To cheesy moments we love the most!

Crusty Conversations

On a table where crust meets fate,
We chat and chew; oh, isn't it great?
Thoughts slide like cheese on a warm pie,
In every nibble, friendships fly high.

A heated debate on the right toppings,
Pineapple fans cause playful stoppings.
Each word crispy, each joke well-baked,
These witty slices cannot be faked.

Saucy tales of food adventures past,
In this room, the joy holds fast.
With grease-stained napkins and smiles so wide,
We savor the moments, side by side.

As laughter rises with every slice,
A crusty bond, oh so precise.
With each shared pie, we find a theme,
In every layer, a cozy dream.

Embracing the Savory

Oh, the warm aroma fills the air,
In a cheesy embrace, we shed our care.
Each crusty edge, a fortress built,
To guard against hunger, to conquer guilt.

With each bite taken, we're transported far,
To a land of flavors where dreams are stars.
A heaping of toppings, an ocean of sauce,
In this kingdom of pizza, we're all the boss.

We conquer our fears with each savory taste,
Creating a world, no bite goes to waste.
Doughy adventures and memories made,
In this culinary dance, we're unafraid.

A slice, a hug, a moment divine,
Tender feelings in every line.
So let's embrace what's warm and round,
In the oven of laughter, true love is found.

A Feast of Tomorrow

Tonight's the night where dreams come true,
Each slice a wish, fresh and new.
With toppings piled high, what's your game?
In this pizza party, we share the fame.

Tomorrow's troubles, let them wait,
For now we feast 'til it feels like fate.
As we dig in, let our hearts be light,
In every bite, we take flight.

The clock ticks on, yet we stand still,
Moments like this give a hearty thrill.
With each savory morsel, our spirits soar,
A banquet of dreams, who could ask for more?

So raise a slice to the joy we make,
In this realm of cheese, don't hesitate.
Tomorrow's worries can stack up high,
But tonight, dear friends, let's reach for the sky!

Pepperoni Dreams

In a world of dough and cheese,
I dream of toppings, if you please.
With pepperoni dancing bright,
Each slice a little slice of light.

Sauce so rich, it sings a song,
As my cravings dance along.
A cheesy grin, I can't resist,
In pizza's warmth, I'm over the moon and blissed.

Crust so crispy, it's divine,
With every bite, a taste of wine.
To share a pie or keep it near,
In every slice, I shed a tear.

As I savor every layer,
Life's too short, don't be a player.
In the kitchen, I twirl and spin,
Crafting dreams where pizza wins!

The Flavorful Journey

On a quest for cheese galore,
From the oven, pizza's lore.
Sausage dreams with a twist of fate,
In every bite, I celebrate.

A slice of fun, a dash of pepper,
With friends around, it couldn't be better.
Garlic knots and salads sing,
In this party, I am the king.

Saucy tales and crusty lore,
Every pie opens a new door.
Exploring flavors, oh so grand,
With a slice, life's a band.

So grab a plate, don't be shy,
With a pizza pie, we fly high.
Adventure awaits, it's clear to see,
In every bite, joy's the key!

A Warm Slice of Joy

In the box, a treasure glows,
Warm and cheesy, oh how it grows.
Each slice whispers, let's have fun,
Under the moon, we'll weigh a ton.

Tomato sauce like a sunset red,
Twirling pasta dreams in my head.
Gather 'round, let laughter rise,
With every bite, the world's a prize.

Garlic sprinkled, dreams unfold,
In pizza's arms, I find pure gold.
The crust, a canvas, stretched so wide,
Creativity rides the cheesy tide.

So lift your slice, raise it high,
In this happy moment, let's testify.
With pizza love, our hearts align,
In this cheesy world, everything's fine!

Cravings Beneath the Stars

Under stars, we gather round,
With heavenly slices, joy is found.
A sprinkle of dreams on every dish,
To savor each bite, that's the wish.

Beneath the moon, stories we share,
A cheesy blanket, without a care.
With every topping, laughter flows,
In this pizza paradise, anything goes.

Crusty whispers, crusty fun,
With each bite, the night's begun.
As stars twinkle in the skies,
Pizza magic, oh how it flies.

So let's enjoy this flavor ride,
With a slice of joy at our side.
Beneath the stars, we make a toast,
To pizza dreams, we love the most!

www.ingramcontent.com/pod-product-compliance
Lightning Source LLC
Chambersburg PA
CBHW072148200426
43209CB00051B/871